Fundamentalism

Alex Woolf

HODDER
Wayland

f Hodder Children's Books

Published in Great Britain in 2003 by Hodder Wayland, a division of Hodder Children's Books.

This book was prepared for Hodder Wayland by Patience Coster at Book Factory.

Series design: Simon Borrough

British Library Cataloguing in Publication Data
Woolf, Alex
Fundamentalism. - (Ideas of the modern world)
1. Religious fundamentalism - Juvenile literature
I. Title
291.1'7

ISBN 0 7502 4366 X

Printed in Hong Kong by Wing King Tong

Hodder Children's Books
A division of Hodder Headline Limited,
338 Euston Road, London NW1 3BH

Acknowledgements
The author and publishers thank the following for permission to reproduce photographs:

The Bridgeman Art Library: pages 8 (Archives Charmet), 29 (Index); Chapel Studios: page 50; Corbis: pages 7, 10, 12, 18, 21, 25, 56-7; Popperfoto: pages 6 (Reuters/Popperfoto/ Jorge Silva), 15, 17, 26-7, 31, 36, 43, 47; Popperfoto/Reuters: pages 4, 24, 38, 41, 42, 48, 49, 51, 52, 53, 58, 59; Rex: pages 22 (SIPA/Rex), 23 (SIPA/Rex), 37 (SIPA/Rex), 44 (ACT); Peter Sanders: page 32; Topham Picturepoint: pages 9 (Topham/Photri), 13, 20 and title page (Tony Savino/The ImageWorks), 30, 35 (Topham/Associated Press), 45 (Topham/Associated Press), 46 (Topham/The ImageWorks), 55 (Topham/Associated Press).

Contents

What is Fundamentalism?

In its strictest sense, fundamentalism means a belief in the **literal** truth of a sacred text. Put another way, fundamentalists believe that the words of the holy book of their religion are the exact truth and are not open to different interpretations. In everyday English, the word 'fundamentalist' is often used to describe someone who is very strict or **conservative** in his or her beliefs.

Fundamentalists are found in all the world's major religions. They are people who care deeply about the traditions of their religion, and they strongly oppose any attempts to reform it or bring it into line with modern thinking. They believe that theirs is the only true religion, and tend to be intolerant of the beliefs of others.

The term 'fundamentalism' originated in America in the early part of the twentieth century, and was used to describe a movement within the Protestant

In January 2002 women in Pakistan chant slogans, demanding the release of imprisoned Islamic fundamentalist leader, Qazi Hussein Ahmed.

The origin of the term

The term 'fundamentalism' was invented in 1920 by an American journalist and preacher called Curtis Lee Laws. He used it to describe the **anti-modern movement** of American Protestants that had emerged since the end of the nineteenth century. Between 1910 and 1915 a leading group of Protestant churchmen had published a series of twelve pamphlets entitled *The Fundamentals of the Faith*, which inspired the term fundamentalism. These pamphlets claimed that there were several fundamentals of Church **doctrine** (principles forming the basis of a belief) that all Christians must believe in. These included the infallibility of the **Bible**, the sinfulness of man, the virgin birth of Jesus, and man's **salvation** through his death. Curtis Lee Laws described fundamentalists as those 'who still cling to the great fundamentals and who mean to do battle royal' for the Christian faith.

Church. Since the 1980s, the meaning of the term has been broadened to include religious movements of other faiths. Not all of these movements believe in the literal truth of a sacred text, yet they share many of the other qualities of fundamentalism, and so have been described as fundamentalist.

In this book we will look at the phenomenon of fundamentalism, examining what the different movements have in common, what causes them to arise and their impact on society. We will also look at specific forms of fundamentalism – particularly Christian and Islamic – discussing their history, present-day significance, and possible future development.

The characteristics of fundamentalism

Fundamentalist movements from different religions – and even from within the same religion – vary greatly. Their particular nature is dependent on the traditions and culture of the religion and society from which they sprang. However, they do tend to have certain characteristics in common.

As has been said, most fundamentalists believe in what they interpret as the literal truth of their particular sacred text, whether it be the Christian Bible, the Muslim Qur'an or the Jewish **Torah**. They consider every sentence of that text to be fact, and not a story or a myth. In their view, the text comes straight from God, and is perfect and never wrong. Because of this, they often want laws and principles within that text enforced throughout society.

Jewish men reading the Torah. Jews believe that the Torah is God's teaching to the Jewish people, telling them how to live and behave. The Torah also contains stories about Jewish history and the Jews' relationship with God.

Fundamentalists are often strongly opposed to anything that contradicts their interpretation of God's laws, especially with regard to matters of human relationships and the family. They tend to be against the idea of equal status for women and men, homosexuality and abortion. They see these things as symptoms of a general decline in society.

It is common for fundamentalists to believe in an ideal time in the past – a golden age – when people lived according to God's laws. And they see

> Randall Terry, founder of Operation Rescue, a **militant** Christian fundamentalist group opposed to abortion, said on 16 August 1993:
>
> *'I want you to just let a wave of intolerance wash over you. I want you to let a wave of hatred wash over you. Yes, hate is good.... Our goal is a Christian nation. We have a Biblical duty, we are called by God, to conquer this country.'*

themselves at the forefront of the struggle to restore that golden age. For Protestants, this perfect time existed during the period of the early Church, while for Muslims it occurred in seventh-century Arabia during the lifetime of the Prophet Muhammad.

The causes of fundamentalism

Fundamentalist movements tend to happen when a religion is perceived to be under threat. One of the main threats to religion today – and the principal cause of the current upsurge in fundamentalism around the world – is that society in general has become more secular (not concerned with religious matters). The role of religion in society has changed from that of a central guiding principle of government and law to a matter of personal choice. This process, known as **secularism**, has occurred at different times and speeds around the world. It occurred in the Christian West in the eighteenth and nineteenth centuries, and in the Muslim world in the nineteenth and twentieth centuries.

Randall Terry delivering a sermon. Fundamentalist groups are often led by a charismatic individual – someone who articulates their desires and fears, and guides their thinking.

This medieval painting shows a story from the Bible in which Jesus fed five thousand people with just five loaves of bread and two fishes. Many Christians believe that the miraculous tales in the Bible really happened, even though they defy scientific explanation.

One early Protestant fundamentalist preacher, John Roach Straton (1875-1929), pointed to the latest scientific knowledge as evidence for the existence of God:

'The whole great machine that we call the universe seems to move with a precision and accuracy that is staggering to the finite mind.... In the realm of physics and chemistry, the same unvarying system is discovered.... What does it all mean? It manifestly means, for one thing, that God has a mission and a designed place for every atom of matter and every ounce of physical force in the entire universe.'

The dominance of Western culture in the world today means that most regions and religions have been affected by secularism. Some people, frustrated at how their community can lose touch with traditional religious principles, have formed fundamentalist movements as a way of opposing secularism.

The challenge of science

Secularism has led to other threats to religion – and causes of fundamentalism – such as science. Science presents a major challenge to religion because it offers people an alternative way of looking at the world, based on reason rather than faith. Science teaches people about the natural causes of events. In matters of health, it has led many people to put their trust in medical procedures and solutions rather than religion.

Science also appears to disprove, or cast into doubt, parts of the 'never-wrong' sacred texts. For example, scientific discoveries have shown that the Earth is a lot older than the Christian Bible implies. And a theory first put forward in the nineteenth century suggests that humans were not created in their present form – as in the story of Adam and Eve – but may have developed from earlier life forms.

Secularism can also lead to changes in society, including a breaking down of the traditional roles played by men and women. In Western countries, women now have the same education and career opportunities as men. They have more control about when to have babies because of the availability of contraception and, if necessary, abortion. Some Christian fundamentalists in the West would like women not to pursue careers but to be simply wives and mothers. In other more religious societies where traditional **gender roles** still apply, fundamentalists fiercely oppose allowing women freedom and equality in the way they live their lives.

Under the fundamentalist Taleban regime of Afghanistan (1995-2001), women were not allowed to go out without wearing a burka, which covered every part of their body. Girls could not go to school, and women were not permitted to work.

Christian Fundamentalism

Christian fundamentalism is for the most part an American movement. Its roots can be traced to the mid-eighteenth century. Between the 1730s and 1770s, the American colonies (which would later become the USA, but at that time were controlled by Britain) experienced an upsurge of religious feeling known as the First Great Awakening. Preachers were at the forefront of the movement, delivering powerful and theatrical sermons intended to scare people into being good Christians by evoking frightening images of Hell. They stressed the powerlessness of humans to achieve **salvation** without the intervention of God.

Jonathan Edwards (1703-58) was one of the most fiery preachers from the First Great Awakening. Here is an excerpt from one of his sermons:

'The God that holds you over the pit of hell, much as one holds a spider, or some loathsome insect over the fire, abhors [hates] you, and is dreadfully provoked... you are ten thousand times more abominable in his eyes, than the most hateful venomous serpent is in ours.... O sinner! Consider the fearful danger you are in: it is... a wide and bottomless pit, full of the fire of wrath, that you are held over in the hand of that God.'

Born again

The First Great Awakening was followed, at the beginning of the nineteenth century, by a new movement called the Second Great Awakening.

George Whitefield (1714-1770) was one of the most famous preachers of the First Great Awakening. It was said that his voice could be heard a mile away, and his open-air sermons attracted crowds of up to 100,000.

What is Christianity?

Christians are followers of Jesus of Nazareth, a Jewish preacher and healer who lived in the Roman province of Palestine around the first century CE. Christians believe that Jesus is the Son of God, who chose to take human form to save people from sin and bring them back to God. After Jesus' death, his followers travelled far and wide and encouraged many to convert to the new religion. Accounts of his life and teachings, as well as the acts and writings of his early followers, make up the New Testament of the **Bible**.

There are many different traditions within Christianity, usually called Churches. These have arisen through disagreements about the teachings, and different ways of worshipping. In the eleventh century, Christianity split into the Orthodox Church and the Catholic Church. By the sixteenth century, many in the Catholic Church believed it had become corrupt and a new movement, known as Protestantism, broke away from it.

From the beginning, Protestantism was never one movement, but was made up of several denominations (groups), including Lutherans, Anglicans and Calvinists. Other Protestant denominations have been established since, including Methodists, Episcopalians, Baptists, Presbyterians and Quakers.

Today Christianity is the largest of all the world's faiths with a total membership of almost two billion. There have been attempts to bring the Christian traditions closer together, and some have reunited. However, new traditions are also arising in many parts of the world.

This was a more optimistic movement, which suggested that humans could save themselves by their own moral actions, the renouncing of sin, and surrender to God. This was called being 'born again'.

The 1830s and 1840s witnessed the emergence of the American **millenarian movement**. The millenarians believed that every word of the Bible was true, and that, according to the Biblical Book of Revelation, the second coming of Jesus Christ would soon occur, to be followed by a thousand years of peace, known as 'the millennium'.

By the end of the nineteenth century, the Church was facing challenges on all sides. The rapid growth in the manufacturing industry, known as the **Industrial Revolution**, had led millions of people to move to the cities in search of jobs. Communities which had traditionally been based around their local church were broken up, and consequently Christianity began to lose its dominant place in people's lives. Education, healthcare and welfare, which had previously been controlled by the Church, became the responsibility of governments. A rising tide of **immigrants** brought other religions, particularly Roman Catholicism, to America. These religions challenged Protestantism as the nation's dominant **creed**.

Faith came to be seen more as a matter of personal choice than something to be enforced by governments and law courts. With the Church no longer so influential as a guide to people's thinking and behaviour, social attitudes also changed. People began to challenge traditional views, for example about the role of women. Many Protestants, fearful of the threats to their traditions, joined the millenarian movement. They were particularly disturbed by the new field of biblical criticism in which scholars studied the Bible as if it were any other ancient text, and not the authoritative word of God.

Harry Emerson Fosdick, a liberal Protestant minister, was a central figure in the fundamentalist debate of the 1920s. His anti-fundamentalist sermon 'Shall the Fundamentalists Win?', delivered in 1922, caused an uproar and led to his resignation in 1925.

In 1902, the millenarians joined with others who believed in the **literal** truth of the Bible, to form the American Bible League with the aim of promoting the Bible as a sacred work, immune to criticism. Millenarians also participated in the writing of the twelve pamphlets entitled *The Fundamentals of the Faith* which led to the coining of the term 'fundamentalism'. In 1919, the millenarians changed their name to the World's Christian Fundamentals Association (WCFA) and, by 1921, they had become known simply as fundamentalists. The WCFA acted as an umbrella organization for fundamentalists from different groupings within the Protestant faith. It lasted until the 1940s.

This 1874 cartoon compares Charles Darwin to an ape. Many believed, wrongly, that Darwin had claimed humans were descended from apes.

The evolution controversy

During the 1920s, the major focus of fundamentalist anger was the teaching of the **theory of evolution** in schools. This was a theory first developed in the nineteenth century by the biologist Charles Darwin, who claimed that human beings, and other creatures, evolved from earlier animals through a process known as '**natural selection**'. According to this theory, humans are part of a family of animals known as **primates**, which includes apes, with whom we share a common ancestor.

Dwight Lyman Moody (1837-99)

Moody, a leading figure in the millenarian movement, left his family's farm at the age of seventeen to go to work in Boston, Massachusetts. While there he converted to Evangelicalism, a form of Protestantism that believes in the authority of the Bible and salvation through personal acceptance of Christ. In 1860, having moved to Chicago, he gave up his business in order to do charitable work in the city slums. Moody was a powerful and intense **orator**, whose sermons stressed a literal interpretation of the Bible, and looked forward to the second coming of Christ. He loathed the trend of biblical criticism and the theory of evolution.

The theory of evolution was a complete contradiction of the Book of Genesis in the Bible, which tells that God created the first humans – Adam and Eve – in His own image. Many people at this time – not just fundamentalists – found it deeply distasteful to hear that, far from being created in the likeness of God, we were descended from ape-like creatures. The fundamentalists were therefore able to recruit many supporters to their cause.

Fundamentalists campaigned throughout the 1920s against the teaching of evolution. They pressurized politicians in eleven states to introduce **legislation** forbidding any teaching that contradicted the biblical view of creation. They succeeded in one state – Tennessee. In 1925, a science teacher named John Scopes, from Dayton, Tennessee was taken to court for teaching about evolution. The fundamentalists won the case, but the reports of the trial in the newspapers ridiculed the fundamentalists' literal interpretation of the Bible.

A period of consolidation

During the 1930s and 1940s, the fundamentalists faded from the national spotlight, as they focused less on political campaigning and more on developing their institutions. Many fundamentalists broke away from their denominations to found new churches. They also established Bible institutes (schools that teach courses in the

The Scopes trial

During the hot summer of 1925, the attention of the world was focused on the trial in a Tennessee courtroom of the high school teacher John T. Scopes. It promised to be a dramatic showdown between fundamentalist believers in the Biblical story of creation, and supporters of Darwin's theory of evolution. The prosecution case was argued by the famous **Democrat** politician and fundamentalist orator, William Jennings Bryan. Trial lawyer Clarence Darrow led for the defence. Darrow repeatedly humiliated Bryan by forcing him to confront apparent contradictions in the supposedly literal truth of the Biblical text. However, the judge would not allow these arguments to stand, and limited the trial to the single question: did Scopes teach evolution? No one could argue that he didn't, and Scopes was found guilty and fined $100. The law banning the teaching of evolution in Tennessee was eventually repealed in 1967.

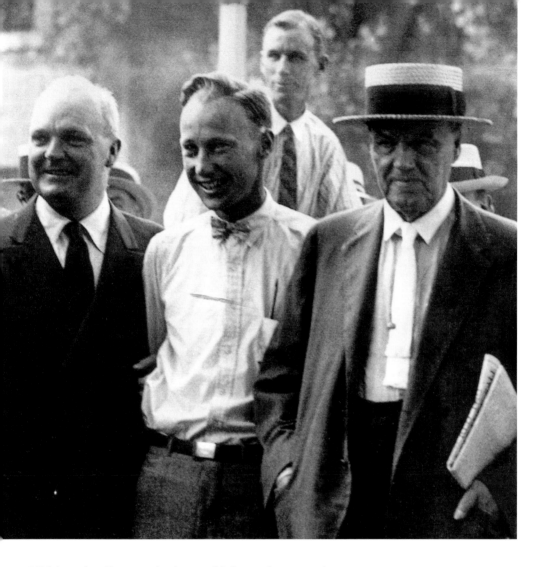

John Scopes, the biology teacher, charged with illegally teaching the theory of evolution, on his way into court with his defence lawyer, Clarence Darrow (wearing a hat).

Bible) and colleges, which would form the central institutions of modern Christian fundamentalism. As well as teaching students, many of these schools also published periodicals, hosted conferences, and started their own radio stations.

To keep themselves separate from the corrupting influences of liberal America, fundamentalists created a whole set of institutions that paralleled the professional and business organizations of society. Students, teachers, doctors, scientists, social workers and businessmen with fundamentalist views could all join fundamentalist groups that specialized in their interest or occupation.

Communism

During the 1950s, fundamentalism re-emerged as a political force, mainly because of the growing fear of communism that overtook the USA for much of that decade. Communism was a political movement that believed in the overthrow of capitalism (the economic system that operated in the West) by means of a working-class revolution. Communist revolutionaries had taken power in Russia in 1917, renaming it the Soviet Union. By the late 1940s the Soviet Union had grown to rival the USA in terms of military power, and communism had attracted many supporters in Europe and, to a lesser extent, in America. Many Americans feared the spread of communism and the threat it posed to their way of life.

For fundamentalists, the most worrying aspect of communism was its rejection of God and religion. Communists saw Christianity and other faiths simply as a way of keeping the working classes in their place. Karl Marx, an early communist thinker, called religion 'the opium of the people.' For this reason above all, fundamentalists regarded communism as an evil that it was their duty to oppose.

It is certainly true that communists saw many of the institutions of Western society, such as the family and religion, as part of the **exploitative** system they wished to replace. However, communism was never as strong in the USA as those who opposed it claimed. Anti-communism was used more as a convenient way of rallying people to the cause of fundamentalism.

Right: Billy Graham preaching in 1954. Graham's crusades have taken him to Europe, Africa, Russia and the Far East. He is said to have preached about Jesus Christ to more people than any other person in history.

The Evangelicals

During the 1950s, fundamentalists were divided on how best to carry forward their message. Some wished to remain separate from modern society, which they saw as sinful and beyond salvation, and to live and work within the alternative institutions they had

16

created. Others believed that it was important to mix with the world, while remaining true to their fundamental Christian beliefs.

This second group called themselves Evangelicals (a revival of an old nineteenth-century movement). Like the preachers of the Second Great Awakening, Evangelicals believed that anyone could find salvation by leading a moral life – for example, by praying and reading the Bible, and by not smoking or drinking alcohol – and through a personal conversion or **baptism**, which they called being 'born again'.

William Franklin Graham (1918-)

The Evangelicals found a champion in a young Baptist evangelist called Billy Graham. His popularity with the wider public and his great skills as an orator helped to get the Evangelical movement noticed and made its arguments more convincing. Graham went on long preaching tours, known as crusades, and regularly appeared on radio and, later, television. As his fame spread, he became friendly with several US presidents, but he always avoided speaking on political issues. This politically 'neutral' stance helped to widen his appeal.

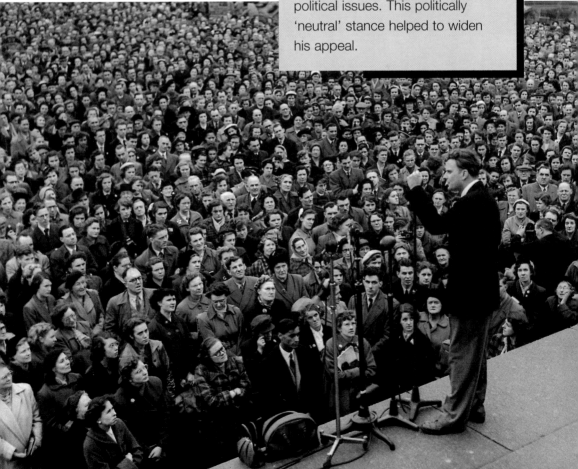

The 1960s was a decade of material wealth but also of increasing consciousness about social inequalities. It was a time of student protests, the anti-war movement, and women's rights. The Evangelicals were particularly outspoken in their opposition to these trends. They campaigned fiercely against the newly available contraceptive pill, the notion of gender equality, and the toleration of homosexuality.

Followers of preacher and broadcaster, Carl McIntire.

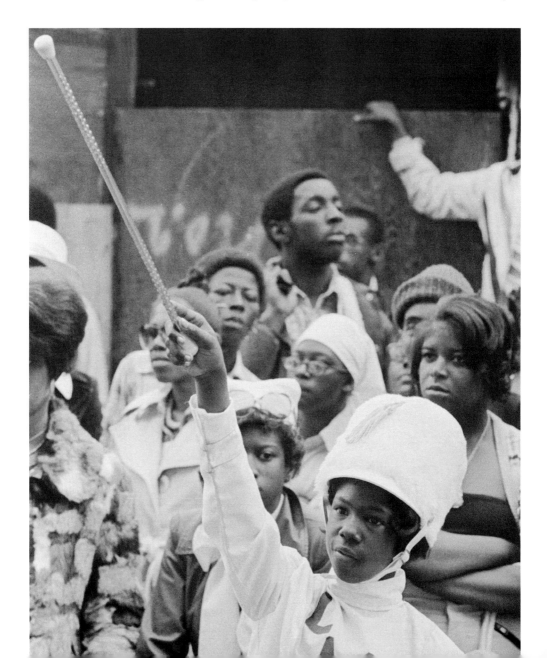

Unlike the fundamentalists, the Evangelicals were happy to work with non-Protestant **conservatives** in their campaigns. For this reason they did not always use religious language to justify their position, but characterized it as a general concern for the erosion of 'family values'. Their strong stand brought them much support from the Protestant community, and many left the established churches to join them. This caused a drop in membership in ten of the largest Protestant denominations (groupings within the Church) during the late 1960s.

The Evangelical movement was much broader and more open than the Christian fundamentalist movement, and it had an international following through the World Evangelical Fellowship, formed in 1951. Evangelicals regularly cooperated with Jews and Roman Catholics in their campaigns in defence of family values. Although the Evangelical movement contained many fundamentalists, it also had members with more liberal views on social issues. Some Evangelicals, while continuing to believe that the Bible was the word of God, became open to modern biblical criticism and even accepted Darwin's controversial theory of evolution.

During the late 1970s and the 1980s, Christian fundamentalists abandoned their separatism, and began once more to engage themselves in the political and social debates of the day. Unlike earlier fundamentalists, who denied themselves luxuries, this new generation was not ashamed of making and spending money, and saw nothing sinful in fast cars and expensive clothing.

Carl McIntire (1907-2002)

Carl McIntire was a leading fundamentalist for more than fifty years. Unlike many Evangelicals, McIntire remained true to the fundamentalist cause throughout his life, and never softened his message to appeal to people outside the movement. The main targets of his fierce rhetoric were communism, **liberalism**, **racial integration**, sex education, and evolution. He reached his peak of popularity during the 1960s with his daily half-hour radio programme, *Twentieth-Century Reformation Hour*, which was broadcast to six hundred stations in the USA and Canada.

In addition to their conservative views on issues of sex and relationships, the new fundamentalists became more outspoken on economic and political issues. They pressed for low taxation, reduced spending on welfare, and increased spending on defence. From the beginning of the 1980s it became difficult to separate the fundamentalists from the Evangelicals, and the two terms are now often used interchangeably.

Christian fundamentalists protesting outside a bookstore against the sale of 'pornographic' books.

The Moral Majority

In the late 1970s, a new movement emerged uniting conservatives of all kinds, from Christian fundamentalists to Catholics and Jews. Its purpose was to encourage millions of ordinary conservative Americans to become involved in the political process. The movement was called the Moral Majority, and it was led by a popular fundamentalist preacher named Jerry Falwell. Through Falwell's television channel, campaign rallies, and mass mailings, thousands of people were persuaded to become politically active.

Voter registration drives brought many people who previously hadn't voted on to the electoral register. Voters were told about a politician's previous record on a range of issues important to religious conservatives – such as abortion, equal rights for women, and school prayer – and they were guided on which way to vote. The Moral Majority scored a major success in 1980 by helping Republican candidate Ronald Reagan win the US presidency. However, once in office, Reagan did little to promote the fundamentalist agenda.

Televangelist Jim Bakker, founder of the PTL (Praise The Lord) network, with his former wife, Tammy Faye. In 1987 his adulterous affair with a church secretary became national news, and in 1989 he was convicted of financial fraud and went to prison for five years.

Televangelism

In the early 1960s, the first Christian television networks appeared in the USA, giving a nationwide platform for Evangelical and fundamentalist preachers. Among the first preachers to see the potential of television were Billy Graham and Oral Roberts, an evangelist and faith healer who appeared to heal people live on television.

Televangelism reached its heyday in the early 1980s. By this time there were more than a hundred religious programmes on television, and the more successful ones were broadcast on two hundred or more television stations around the country. Popular televangelists such as Jerry Falwell and Pat Robertson could reach millions with their programmes, and this made them politically powerful. Much airtime was devoted to fundraising, and many televangelists became very wealthy as a result. Towards the end of the 1980s, a series of financial and sexual scandals involving televangelists threatened to tarnish the whole industry. However, the arrival of satellite and cable TV in the 1990s lowered the cost of airtime and gave religious broadcasting a new lease of life.

During the 1980s, the conservatives dominated the political scene, and it became harder for the Moral Majority to find reasons to raise funds from its supporters. Having won the battle to control the government, their supporters saw less need to continue making donations. In 1987, Falwell dissolved the Moral Majority, and retired from political activism. His place as the nation's leading fundamentalist was taken by Pat Robertson, a **Pentecostal** minister and televangelist.

The Christian Coalition

Rather than trying to influence the political scene from the sidelines, Robertson decided to run for president himself, representing the conservative Republican Party. He had a huge base of support through his Christian Broadcasting Network, and access to plentiful funds. However, despite spending more money than any other candidate, Robertson failed to get any nominations from his own party to be the Republican presidential candidate. After this defeat, Robertson focused on building the Christian Coalition, an organization similar to the Moral Majority. By 1992, it claimed to have 350,000 members. During the 1990s, the Christian Coalition tried hard to make the Republican Party more

Pat Robertson campaigning for the US presidency in 1988. Many fundamentalists were uncomfortable with his mixing of religion and politics. In one poll of conservative Christians, 42 per cent said that his status as a former clergyman made them less likely to vote for him.

A gay rights march in Washington DC. Christian fundamentalists are fiercely opposed to giving homosexuals the same rights as heterosexual couples, such as the right to marry or adopt children.

supportive of its beliefs on moral issues. It spent a lot of money backing candidates with conservative views, and managed to get several elected. However, Christian Coalition candidates failed in 1992, 1996, and in 2000, to win the Republican nomination for the US presidency.

From an interview given by Jerry Falwell on 14 September 2001, three days after the terrorist attack on the World Trade Centre in New York claimed thousands of lives:

'The ACLU [American Civil Liberties Union] has got to take a lot of blame for this. And I know I'll hear from them for this, but throwing God... out of the public square, out of the schools, the abortionists have got to bear some burden for this because God will not be mocked, and when we destroy 40 million little innocent babies, we make God mad.... I really believe that the pagans and the abortionists and the feminists and the gays and the lesbians who are actively trying to make that an alternative lifestyle, the ACLU, People for the American Way, all of them who try to secularize America.... I point the thing in their face and say – you helped this happen.'

The main aims of most modern Christian fundamentalists can be stated as follows: they want abortion and homosexuality banned, and women to take up what they see as their traditional roles as wives and mothers; in schools they want compulsory public prayer, the story of creation to be taught, and the teaching of evolution to be banned.

To achieve these aims, fundamentalists have raised and spent a lot of money, encouraged thousands to become politically active, supported election campaigns, **lobbied** politicians, and fought court cases. But their impact on US politics and culture has been slight. Despite hard campaigning by the fundamentalists, abortion remains legal in the USA, although in some states it requires parental consent for those under the age of eighteen and the time period within which it must be carried out is more restricted.

In 1997 members of the Evangelical Christian group the Promise Keepers lie face down in prayer at a religious gathering in view of the Washington Monument in Washington DC.

Prayers in school – another regular campaigning issue for the fundamentalists – have been judged to be against the US **constitution**. Evolution also continues to be taught in schools throughout the USA, despite numerous court cases in which fundamentalists have tried to argue that it should be banned or given equal classroom time with '**creation science**'.

Individual liberty

Christian fundamentalism's failure to change the USA has a lot to do with the nature of the country and its people. The USA is a **democratic** nation, containing many diverse cultures, and it is generally united around certain values, including the liberty of the individual. This places the country at odds with the fundamentalists, who would like all Americans to accept their beliefs on how people should live, behave and worship.

It is interesting to note that in a poll of voting patterns in the southern states during the 1988 campaign for the Republican nomination for president, only 14 per cent of conservative Christians voted for Pat Robertson. This suggests that while many Americans are deeply religious, most seem happy to keep religion a private matter.

Oral Roberts (1918-)

Oral Roberts was one of the most famous and controversial evangelical preachers of the twentieth century. During the 1940s he began his 'crusades for Christ', in which he set himself the target of 'winning a million souls for Christ' each year. In 1954, he bought time on US television to display his gift of faith healing. Many sick people did appear to be healed when he laid his hands on them. This led him into conflicts with the fundamentalists, who accused him of trivializing their cause. Roberts grew increasingly wealthy from fundraising campaigns supposedly for charitable causes. During the 1980s, he claimed that Jesus had told him he would die if his supporters did not give him eight million dollars in the next twelve months. The money was apparently raised, and Roberts survived.

Oral Roberts has always been a controversial figure, even among fundamentalists – many of whom do not believe in his miracle cures.

Islamic Fundamentalism

Islamic fundamentalism has several characteristics in common with Christian fundamentalism. Islamists, as the fundamentalists prefer to call themselves, choose to interpret their holy book, the Qur'an, literally. They wish to enforce the laws contained in the Qur'an, known as the *shari'ah*, on Islamic society. They are strict about the laws that forbid the drinking of alcohol and believe that women should not work or be educated, and should wear a veil in public.

Islamists reject many of the traditions and customs that developed within Islam during the Medieval period as a betrayal of the true faith. Much like Christian fundamentalists, they wish to return to a purer form of their religion, as it existed in its earliest days. Like the Evangelicals, Islamists emphasize the importance of being 'converted' to true Islam, and they believe in the importance of **missionary** work.

Islamic fundamentalists are not all the same. Some, like the Saudi-born terrorist Osama bin Laden, believe in bringing together all Muslim peoples in a restoration of the '**caliphate**' – a united Islamic world under one central leadership. Others, like the Palestinian organization Hamas, wish to create an Islamic republic (a country ruled by Islamic religious leaders) in just one country – in their case, Palestine. In fundamentalist Iran, women drive cars and go to work, whereas in Afghanistan, under the fundamentalist Taleban regime (1995–2001), women had no such rights. There are different kinds of fundamentalism in Islam, but there are also enough similarities to make it a single, coherent movement.

Muslims gathering for prayers in Delhi, India, at the festival of Eid ul-Fitr, marking the end of Ramadan, the month of fasting.

What is Islam?

Islam was founded by an Arabian merchant named Muhammad in the seventh century AD. Muslims believe that Muhammad was the last in a line of prophets such as Moses and Jesus whose message came straight from God (*Allah* in Arabic). They believe that Allah passed on his message to Muhammad in the words of the Qur'an, the holy scripture of Islam. The Qur'an contains teachings about God, justice and daily life, as well as Islamic versions of stories also found in the **Bible**. Muslims express their faith in actions carried out each day, for example by praying five times a day, fasting during the Muslim month of **Ramadan**, and going on a pilgrimage to the holy city of Mecca at least once in a lifetime. Islam is a complete way of life, influencing how believers eat, dress and behave. For example, Muslims can only eat meat slaughtered in a certain way. They cannot drink alcohol or gamble, and they must dress modestly.

The origins of Islamic fundamentalism

From time to time in its development, Islam has faced crises, and these have usually been followed by attempts to return Islamic society to its original principles based on the teachings of the Qur'an. These are called **revivalist movements**. The origins of Islamic fundamentalism lie in these attempts at revival.

The first of the important revivalist movements occurred in the late thirteenth and early fourteenth centuries, and was inspired by the teachings of Ahmad ibn Taymiyya (1263-1328). He was born soon after the invasion of the Middle East (where Arab Muslims lived) by an Asian people called the Mongols.

Different traditions of Islam

During the mid-seventh century, a division occurred in Islam when Ali, who was Muhammad's son-in-law, became the fourth caliph (ruler). One group – the Shi'a, meaning 'partisans' (followers) – believed Ali was Muhammad's first true successor, because of his family relationship to the Prophet. Another group – the Sunni, meaning 'majority' – disagreed. To this day, the Shi'a believe that the caliphate should be **hereditary**, like a dynasty of kings, whereas the Sunni insist that caliphs should be chosen democratically.

From about the eighth century, a more mystical tradition arose in Islam, which became known as Sufism. This tradition emphasized the spiritual side of the faith. Unlike other forms of Islam, the Sufis used music and dance as part of their worship. Many different Sufi orders arose, some of which still survive.

Taymiyya believed that the defeat by the Mongols had occurred because the Arab people had lost touch with Islamic teachings and had become corrupt. He objected to Sufism, for example, a more mystical form of Islam that emphasized the spiritual side of worship. Taymiyya insisted that all such 'un-Islamic' traditions should cease, and that the Muslim world should be run according to the strict interpretation of Islamic law as it appears in the Qur'an.

Wahhabism

By the eighteenth century, the Arab world was dominated by the powerful **Ottoman Empire**, which occupied lands in southern Europe, North Africa, the Middle East and Asia. The Ottoman rulers called themselves caliphs, using the ancient title to give themselves religious authority over the people of their empire. But Sufism was flourishing in many parts of the empire, and many Arabs believed that the Ottoman caliphate was corrupt.

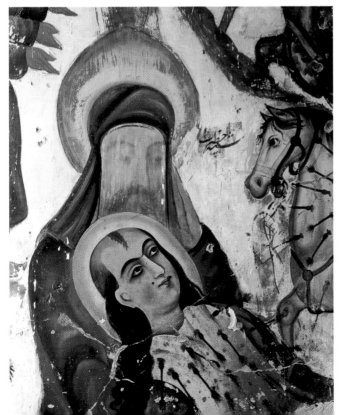

A painting of the fourth caliph, Ali, who was Muhammad's son-in-law. Shi'a Muslims, such as most of those who live in Iran, believe that Ali was Muhammad's first true successor.

Muhammad ibn 'Abd al-Wahhab (1703-92)

Al-Wahhab was born near Riyadh in modern-day Saudi Arabia. He was a bright child, and at the age of ten could recite the whole of the Qur'an from memory. After completing his education at Medina, he lived abroad for many years. On his travels around the Islamic world, al-Wahhab found evidence of differing religious practices, which he viewed as a corruption of the original faith. While a teacher in Iran in 1736, al-Wahhab began to spread his belief about a return to a purer form of Islam. On his return to Medina, he wrote the *Kitab at-tawhid* ('Book of Unity'), which became the main text of the Wahhabi movement. In 1745, he met with Prince Muhammad ibn Sa'ud, who was impressed with al-Wahhab's ideas, and adopted them for his country, Saudi Arabia.

A movement arose in Saudi Arabia known as the Wahhabis, after its founder, Muhammad al-Wahhab. The Wahhabis were opposed to Sufism and Shi'ism (the branch of Islam that believes the caliphate should be hereditary), and sought a return to a purer and more traditional interpretation of the Qur'an. In contrast with the Sufis, the Wahhabis insisted that Allah stood apart from the world, and could not be reached through mystical rituals or **meditation**. They also demanded independence from the caliphate.

Saudi forces carrying the Wahhabi standard in the Arabian desert in 1913. That year they captured the Hasa region of the Arabian peninsula, as part of their campaign to spread Wahhabism to the whole of Arabia.

A major fear of the Wahhabis was progress and change. They believed that the innovations of the modern world – such as the introduction of coffee, tobacco, and printing – endangered the purity of their religion. They looked back on the 'golden age' of Muhammad's time as an ideal period, and they wished to preserve Islamic society as it was then. In their desire to purge Islam of new and foreign influences, the Wahhabis were very similar to modern Islamic fundamentalists, and can be seen as one of the major inspirations for today's movement. Wahhab's teachings were adopted by the Muslim leader and founder of Saudi Arabia, ibn Sa'ud, and **Wahhabism** was spread by conquest to most of Arabia. This strict form of Islam has dominated Saudi Arabia since 1800, making it arguably the world's first Islamic fundamentalist state.

Alexandria in Egypt under British colonial rule (1883-1937). During this period Egyptian Islamic courts declined in power, and were only permitted to deal with cases involving personal relationships.

The Islamic Movement

During the late eighteenth and nineteenth centuries, the Ottoman Empire declined, and European powers, fuelled by the wealth of the **Industrial Revolution**, grew to dominate many parts of the Muslim world. This submission to Western power led to a steady wearing away of Islamic identity.

31

The introduction of Western goods such as modern weapons, railways, and later electricity, running water, and cars, gave many Muslims a taste for Western life and culture. European-style institutions, such as law courts, banks, schools and colleges were introduced in many countries of the Ottoman Empire, in parallel with existing religious institutions. These reforms were not forced on Muslims by Western powers, but carried out by local rulers.

This process of Westernization was opposed by some in religious circles and led, in the 1870s, to a new upsurge in Islamic revivalism. One of the leading figures in this new movement was Jamal al-Afghani (1838-97). Al-Afghani travelled throughout the Islamic world, spreading his anti-Western message. He believed that Western powers like Britain, France and Russia were working with Middle Eastern rulers to exploit the Muslim people and the resources of their countries.

Muhammad Abduh (1849-1905)

Abduh is regarded as one of the major influences behind the modern revival of Islam. In 1899 he was made the official expert in Islamic law in Egypt, and in this position he brought about many reforms. In his writings and actions, Abduh opposed the blind acceptance of traditional customs, and urged a return to the pure faith of early Islam. He called for modernization based on Islamic principles. For example, he believed that girls, as well as boys, should have the right to an education. He also argued that there was nothing un-Islamic about Western technology, so long as it was put to good uses.

Muhammad Abduh as a young man. When he was a student, Abduh became involved in the Islamic Movement. He was exiled from Egypt for six years after taking part in a rebellion against the British in 1882.

In an effort to unite the Muslim world, al-Afghani formed the Islamic Movement. He encouraged the strict observance of Islamic beliefs in everyday life and the reintroduction of *shari'ah* – Islamic law. *Shari'ah* law arises from the teachings of the Qur'an, the **Hadith** (the sayings of Muhammad) and the interpretations of scholars. It is both a personal code for every Muslim, and the system of law governing strict Muslim countries. Al-Afghani also urged Muslims to fight the Western powers, if necessary with the modern weapons and technology the Europeans had introduced. The Islamic Movement aimed to restore the power and status that Islam had enjoyed during the height of the Ottoman Empire. Modern Islamic fundamentalism dates from this time, and is a reaction to the threat of Western economic and cultural domination.

The Ottoman Empire finally collapsed in 1918, following its defeat in the First World War. The caliphate was no more, and the Islamic world found itself without an overall leader. Many countries of the former empire, including Palestine, Iraq, Jordan, Syria and Lebanon, fell under the control of France and Britain. In other places, such as Turkey, Egypt and Iran, independent nations were formed. Here, the new leaders were modernizers who wished to follow the West, and reduce the role of religion. They separated Islam from the state, and replaced religious institutions with **secular** ones.

Al-Afghani, founder of the Islamic Movement, was concerned about the influence of Western materialism on Islam. In 1880 he wrote:

'They [the materialists, influenced by the West] are the destroyers of civilization and the corrupters of morals.... Their kindness is a ruse, their truthfulness a deceit, their claim to humanity imaginary, and their call to science and knowledge a snare and a forgery. They make trustworthiness into treachery; will not keep a secret; and will sell their closest friend for a copper coin. They are slaves to the belly and bound by lust.... Thus, from all we have expounded, it becomes clear... that religion, even if it be false and the basest of religions... is better than the way of the materialists.... The Islamic religion is the only religion that... sets up proofs for each fundamental belief in such a way that it will be useful to all people.'

The Muslim Brotherhood

In the period following the collapse of the Ottoman Empire, various Islamic groups formed to oppose Western dominance and the reforms of the modernizers. One group, which was to have lasting impact, was the Muslim Brotherhood, founded in Egypt in 1928 by Hasan al-Banna. It urged a return to the Qur'an and the Hadith as guides to a successful modern Islamic society. The Brotherhood spread quickly through Egypt, the Sudan, Syria, Palestine and Lebanon, encouraging these countries to re-adopt strict Islamic law.

During the 1950s, leaders of Middle Eastern countries, such as President Nasser of Egypt, discouraged Islamic revivalism. Instead they tried to promote Arab **nationalism** – a sense of identification with Arabic culture (the Arabs are a people living throughout North Africa and the Middle East). The idea was that, if all the Arab nations worked together, they could be strong enough to oppose the West. Communism also became increasingly popular among Arabs at this time, many of whom saw an alliance with the communist Soviet Union as another way to end Western influence.

However, movements such as the Muslim Brotherhood kept the flame of Islamic revivalism burning during this period. One of the Brotherhood's leading theorists was Sayyid Qutb (1906–66). His writings in the early 1960s – especially *In the Shadow of the Qur'an* and *Milestones* – were to be a major influence on radical Muslims in the years to come.

Qutb differed from earlier Islamic thinkers and from many of his

In *Milestones* Sayyid Qutb wrote:

'The faithful Muslim seeks a state where there is 'no sovereignty (authority) except God's, no law except from God, and no authority of one man over another as the authority in all respects belongs to God.'

contemporaries in his view that there was no such thing as Islamic society in today's world. He believed that, since the time of the Prophet, the world had deteriorated into a state of *jahiliyya*, or ignorance. It was the duty of every Muslim to break free of the world, then destroy it, and build a pure Islamic state on its ruins. Qutb was executed by the Egyptian government in 1966 for his political activities.

Qutb's belief that violence was a necessary step towards the creation of a pure Islamic state was later taken up by fellow Egyptian, Abd al-Salam Faraj. Faraj took the Arabic word **jihad**, meaning 'struggle', and redefined it as 'violent struggle' or 'holy war'. He said it was the duty of Muslims to engage in violence against the enemies of Islam. Their reward for doing so would be a place in paradise. Faraj was later executed for his part in the 1981 assassination of President Anwar Sadat of Egypt.

Two imprisoned Islamic militants, accused of the October 1981 assassination of President Anwar Sadat, defiantly hold up copies of the Qur'an. They were executed in April 1982, along with three others.

The Palestinian issue

In 1948, the Jewish state of Israel was established in the former British territory of Palestine. A war immediately erupted between the new nation and neighbouring Arab states opposed to its establishment. Many hundreds of thousands of Palestinian Arabs fled their homes. They settled in refugee camps in Syria, Lebanon, Jordan, and in territories bordering Israel known as the West Bank and the Gaza Strip. From its birth, Israel aroused the hostility of the Arab world. The Arabs were angered by the displacement of the Palestinians from their homeland, and the occupation by a Jewish state of formerly Arab lands and Muslim holy sites. In 1967, in what became known as the Six Day War, Israel defeated a combined Arab attack. As a result of that war, Israel expanded her territory to include the West Bank and the Gaza Strip. These areas became known as the 'occupied territories'.

An Israeli soldier with an Arab prisoner during the 1967 Six Day War. Israel scored a dramatic victory, despite facing simultaneous attack on three fronts by Egypt, Syria and Jordan. The legacy of this brief conflict casts a shadow over the Middle East to this day.

The war, and the subsequent enlargement of Israel, caused widespread anger throughout the Muslim world, and many took up the cause of Palestinian liberation. A group of **militant** Palestinians called the Palestine Liberation Organization (PLO) turned to terrorism in its desire to destroy Israel.

From around 1973, Islamic revivalism, as defined by al-Afghani, Qutb, and other thinkers, began to replace nationalism and communism as the most

influential radical movement of the Muslim world.
The PLO was a secular (not religious) organization,
so militant Islamic Palestinians in the occupied
territories formed their own anti-Israeli terrorist
groups. Most notable among these was Hamas (the
Islamic Resistance Movement), formed in 1978.

The Iranian Revolution

In Iran during the late 1970s the pro-Western,
secular government of Shah Mohammad Reza
Pahlavi faced fierce opposition from the country's
religious leaders, known as the *ayatollahs*. Iranian
Muslims followed the minority Shi'ite tradition of
Islam, and were not regarded as true Muslims by the
Sunni Muslims who form the majority of Muslims
worldwide (see page 28). Nevertheless Iran provided
the setting, in 1979, for a revolution that would
shock the world and begin the major upsurge known
as Islamic fundamentalism that continues to this day.

A pro-Khomeini demonstration at the time of the Iranian Revolution. The revolution succeeded partly because the Shah's government had never been able to suppress the Islamists as other Arab governments had managed. The ayatollahs were also fortunate that the Shah's programme of modernization failed to improve the lives of Iranians.

In 1978, there were riots and demonstrations throughout Iran. In January 1979 the Shah left the country. The opposition movements united under a new leader, Ayatollah Khomeini, then in exile, who took power in February. Khomeini ruthlessly imposed *shari'ah* law (see page 26). All aspects of life, from marriage ceremonies to banking, were made to conform to *shari'ah*. Once their power was consolidated in Iran, the *ayatollahs* tried to export their revolution to neighbouring countries. Iraq, with its large Shi'ite minority, was their first target. However, after a bloody eight-year war (1980-88), Iran finally withdrew.

Members of the terrorist group Hezbollah lined up behind Shi'ite clerics.

Hezbollah

The Iranian fundamentalists also tried unsuccessfully to spark Islamic revolutions in Lebanon, Egypt, Saudi Arabia, Jordan and Algeria. In Lebanon, the Iranians gave their support to a Shi'ite group known as Hezbollah (the 'Party of Allah'). The aim of this group was to conquer Lebanon, and ultimately to create one all-encompassing Islamic state. Hezbollah were among the most single-minded and ruthless of Islamic fundamentalists, willing to give up their lives to kill their enemies. For example, in October 1983,

The Rushdie fatwah

In 1989, Ayatollah Khomeini issued a *fatwah* (religious ruling) that sentenced the Anglo-Indian writer Salman Rushdie to death for blasphemy (showing disrespect to God). This *fatwah* was in response to Rushdie's novel, *The Satanic Verses*, which contains a passage that many Muslims find offensive, about the birth of a religion resembling Islam. Rushdie was forced to go into hiding in case a Muslim decided to carry out the death sentence against him. In 1999, the Iranian government pledged not to continue the *fatwah*. But in 2000 an extremist Iranian group, the Iranian 15th Khordad Foundation, offered a bounty of $2.8 million for Rushdie's execution. And in February 2001, the Islamic Propagation Organization reaffirmed the death sentence on Rushdie. President Khatami of Iran accused these groups of damaging the country's international image. In March 2002, Air Canada banned Salman Rushdie from its flights, saying that the extra security required for him to fly could mean delays of up to three hours for other passengers.

a Hezbollah suicide bomber drove a truck filled with explosives into a barracks in Beirut, killing 241 US Marines and 58 French paratroopers.

The Iranians had shown by example how an Islamic revolution could occur. Their success inspired Islamic militants throughout the world. The 1980s and 1990s was a time of **radicalism** and violence in many Muslim countries, from North Africa to South-East Asia, as increasing numbers of young, eager and committed Muslims flocked to the cause.

In Egypt and Algeria the fundamentalist movements were suppressed, while in Jordan and Pakistan fundamentalist candidates were allowed to compete in elections. In 1989, a fundamentalist regime came to power in Sudan, and another – the Taleban – took control of Afghanistan in 1995 – but these were isolated successes. In most cases, the fundamentalists, for all their ruthlessness and commitment, have been unable to achieve real political power.

Anti-Americanism

The upsurge of modern Islamic militancy has many causes. They include the political and economic failures of the post-independence Arab governments, the Palestinian issue, and the inspirational writings of men such as Sayyid Qutb. But perhaps the most potent force driving Islamic fundamentalism today is anti-Americanism. This is reflected in an increasing number of attacks by Islamic terrorists on American targets. The worst of these were the attacks on 11 September 2001, when aircraft full of innocent passengers were hijacked by members of the terrorist group Al Qaeda, and deliberately flown into the twin towers of the World Trade Centre in New York and the Pentagon near Washington DC. More than 3,000 people were killed.

There are several reasons why the United States has attracted such hatred. As the leading Western power, it has become the modern-day equivalent of the European colonial powers of the nineteenth century (see pages 31-2). Although it has no direct political control over the Islamic world, the USA's influence is felt in terms of its economic power, and its ability to persuade the governments of Muslim countries to act in America's interests.

The Taleban

The Taleban regime in Afghanistan (1995-2001) was notable for its extreme fundamentalist policies. Its members wished to create the world's purest Islamic state, and set about banning all 'corrupting' influences such as TV, music and cinema. They followed a strict interpretation of shari'ah law. Women in particular faced extreme restrictions: they were denied education or the right to work, and were forced to cover themselves from head to foot in a garment called a **burka**. Adultery was punishable by stoning to death, and the hands and feet of thieves were amputated. Those who did not pray five times a day or fast during the Muslim holy month of Ramadan were sent to prison.

Muslims also feel their culture is under threat from the worldwide dominance of American culture, conveyed in the form of movies, television, music, books, food and fashion. They are offended by Western liberal attitudes towards sex, alcohol, drugs and **gender roles**. They view this culture as corrupt, decadent, and completely at odds with Islamic principles. They are also angered by the willingness of their own governments to be corrupted by Western culture.

Many Muslims are also enraged by the USA's policy in the Middle East, especially its support of Israel. Another cause of discontent among religious Muslims is the presence, since 1991, of US troops in the holy land of Saudi Arabia. This has been a particular source of outrage for the Saudi-born terrorist, Osama bin Laden, who is thought to have masterminded the 11 September 2001 attacks. Bin Laden has called upon Muslims to kill Americans – even civilians – for as long as their soldiers remain in Saudi Arabia.

On 11 September 2001, the second hijacked plane crashes into the south tower of the World Trade Centre in New York. The gaping hole in the north tower from the earlier collision can clearly be seen. Soon afterwards both towers collapsed.

A statement made by Osama bin Laden in 1998 contained the following words:

'Nothing is more sacred than belief except repulsing an enemy who is attacking religion and life. On that basis, and in compliance with God's order, we issue the following fatwah to all Muslims. The ruling to kill the Americans and their allies – civilians and military – is an individual duty for every Muslim who can do it in any country in which it is possible to do it.'

Muslim women in Jakarta, Indonesia, demonstrate their support for the introduction of Islamic shari'ah law in August 2002.

Islamic fundamentalism today

Since 1979, Islamic fundamentalism has been a major force for change around the world. It is a cause that has been taken up enthusiastically by young Muslims everywhere, from Bradford in England to Mindanao in the Philippines. In many parts of the Middle East and central and southern Asia, Islamic fundamentalism has had a violent aspect, and caused political instability.

However, Islam is a peaceful religion. Not all Islamists are terrorists, and a substantial number are opposed to terrorist violence of any kind. Islamism, or Islamic revivalism, is seen by many in the Muslim world as a positive force. Groups like the Muslim Brotherhood, although they have been involved with terrorism in the past, are now pursuing their aims by winning power through **democratic** elections. Islamists often see their role as trying to influence Islamic governments towards implementing Islamic laws, and bringing those who have deviated back to the true faith. Despite this, Islamic fundamentalism has become strongly associated with terrorism in the Western mind, as it is violent fundamentalist groups such as Hamas, Hezbollah and Palestinian Islamic Jihad that make the headlines.

Osama bin Laden (1957-)

The son of a wealthy Saudi Arabian businessman, bin Laden developed an early interest in Islam, and at the age of 23 went to help in the resistance to the Soviet invasion of Afghanistan in 1979-88. Here he developed a large network of Islamic militants, which later evolved into the international terrorist group, Al Qaeda.

In the early 1990s, bin Laden's increasingly extreme views brought him into conflict with the Saudi regime. He moved to Sudan, from where he sponsored Islamic terrorist attacks around the world, especially against Saudi and American targets. In 1995, he moved his operation to Afghanistan where Al Qaeda allied itself with the ruling Taleban regime. After the 11 September 2001 attacks by Al Qaeda members, American-led forces toppled the Taleban and destroyed Al Qaeda's bases, although they failed to find bin Laden. He is believed to be either dead or in hiding somewhere in Afghanistan or Pakistan.

Few Muslims agree with bin Laden's violent interpretation of Islam. However, his uncompromising attitude appeals to the poor and frustrated in places like Palestine, Egypt, Sudan, Saudi Arabia and Indonesia. He is willing to cut across the boundaries that divide many Muslims. For example, despite being a Sunni, he made an alliance with the Shi'ite terrorist group, Hezbollah. His ultimate aim is to re-establish the caliphate, and unite Islam into one force. Then, he believes, Islam will be strong enough to defeat the West.

Osama bin Laden's hostility towards the West has made him popular among thousands of Islamic militants worldwide. An audiotape containing what experts believe to be his voice, released in November 2002, suggests that he may still be alive.

Other Forms of Fundamentalism

The long conflict with the Palestinians and Arab nations that has followed the establishment of the state of Israel has affected Jewish people in different ways. Many yearn for a peaceful settlement with the Palestinians, even if that means giving some land back to them. There are others who will accept nothing less than outright victory over the Arabs and refuse to give up an inch of land. The latter group include a religious movement of mainly Israeli Jews who have become known as Jewish fundamentalists.

Jewish fundamentalism

For many centuries, the Jews were without a homeland. In the sixteenth and seventeenth centuries a movement known as **Zionism** emerged, arguing that the Jews should reclaim from the Arabs the land they had possessed in Biblical times. In the nineteenth and twentieth centuries, Zionism became a political rather than religious movement as it sought to create a secular Jewish state.

Yet in the decades since Israel was founded, most fundamentalist Jews have come to view its establishment in religious terms. They see the current **secular** state of Israel as the initial form of the religious 'land of Israel' (*Eretz Yisrael* in Hebrew), which would be governed according to *halakah* (Jewish law). For confirmation of this view, fundamentalists look to the Jewish holy book, the **Torah**, where there is a commandment to return to *Eretz Yisrael*, to settle there and conquer it.

Jewish Zionists believe they have the right to settle anywhere in the occupied territory of the West Bank, which they call by the Biblical names of Judea and Samaria. Many of them carry guns and there are frequent violent clashes with Palestinians.

44

Gush Emunim

Gush Emunim (the Bloc of the Faithful) was a religious Zionist group formed in 1974. The members of this group believed that Israel's 1967 territorial conquests were willed by God, and they were determined that not one inch should be given back. While the Israeli government was facing international pressure to return some of this land to the Palestinians, Gush began settling in the occupied territories in an attempt to make them a permanent part of Israel. During the late 1970s, Gush Emunim became increasingly popular in Israel, and Gush leaders were elected to the Israeli Parliament. Then, when the Israeli government made a peace deal with Egypt, and began handing back land, Gush turned to terrorism, wounding two Palestinian mayors in car bomb attacks in the West Bank in 1980. Another plot to dynamite the **mosques** on a Jewish holy site in Jerusalem was discovered, and in 1984 several Gush members were arrested.

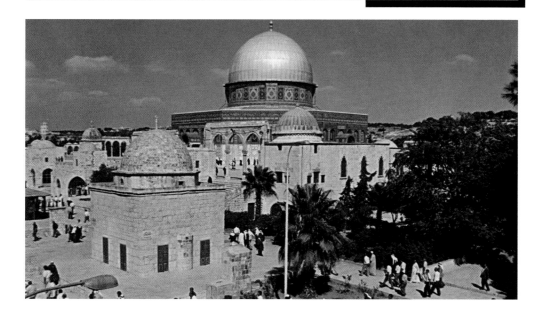

Their view, which is known as religious Zionism, became more popular after Israel's unexpected victory in the 1967 war. As a result, Israel drove back the Arabs and greatly expanded her territory, bringing it roughly into line with the borders of the Biblical land of Israel. To religious Zionists, it appeared that God's will had been done.

Gush Emunim planned to blow up these mosques on the Temple Mount in Jerusalem.

45

The religious Zionists, with their belief in Israel's god-given status, are the driving force behind the movement by Jewish people to settle the occupied territories. Fundamentalists see this not as conquest, but as the reclamation of land that rightfully belongs to them.

Unlike their Muslim and Christian counterparts, Jewish fundamentalists do not seek converts to their extreme cause, except among other Jews. One reason why Jewish fundamentalists do not try to convert non-Jews is that many of them hold racist views towards non-Jews. They regard Jews as superior to Arabs and Christians. This belief stems partly from a Jewish movement, popular between the sixteenth and nineteenth centuries, called the Lurianic Cabbala. One of the main beliefs of this movement was that the world was created solely for the Jews, and that non-Jews have 'satanic souls'.

Jewish settlers from Elon Moreh, near Nablus, carry the body of Rabbi Hillel Lieberman, who was killed in October 2000, probably by Palestinians. Despite the violence, the numbers of Jewish settlers continues to grow at a rate of 5 per cent a year.

Their racist attitudes mean that many Jewish fundamentalists are not troubled by the idea of settling on land previously lived on by Arabs. Some, such as the extremist followers of the **Rabbi** Meir Cahane (who died in 1990), would like to evict Arabs from land in the Middle East which they believe rightfully belongs to Jews. A few even believe that Jews who kill Arabs should not be punished. In February 1994, the Jewish extremist Baruch Goldstein fired his rifle indiscriminately at a crowd of Palestinian worshippers in the Tomb of the Patriarchs in the town of Hebron, killing 29 people. Yet a number of fundamentalists refused to condemn this act as murder.

Jewish fundamentalists justify their acts of violence – even attacks on fellow Jews – by reference to their scriptures. In November 1995, a Jewish fundamentalist called Yigal Amir assassinated the Israeli prime minister Yitzhak Rabin, who had recently signed a peace deal with the Palestinians. Amir claimed his action was justified by the 'law of the pursuer', from the **Talmud** (the book of Jewish law). This law commands every Jew to kill or wound any other Jew who is perceived as intending to kill another Jew. Since, in Amir's view, Rabin was endangering Israel and therefore the lives of Jewish people by his peace deal, Amir felt it was right to kill him. Amir was sentenced to life imprisonment.

Rabbi Kook the Elder, the father of religious Zionism, said:

'The difference between a Jewish soul and souls of non-Jews – all of them in all different levels – is greater and deeper than the difference between a human soul and the souls of cattle.'

(Quoted in Israel Shahak and Norton Mezvinsky, *Jewish Fundamentalism in Israel*.)

Yigal Amir (second right), assassin of Yitzhak Rabin, under arrest. At his trial, Amir said in his defence that Rabin had wanted to 'give our country to the Arabs'. 'We need to be cold-hearted,' he added.

47

Hindu fundamentalism

Hindu fundamentalism differs from other forms of fundamentalism because of the differing nature of the religion. Hindus believe in many gods; they are tolerant of other faiths, and respect their gods. They have several holy books, such as the Vedas, the Bhaghavad Gita and the Ramayana, and do not insist that one book should be regarded as the complete source of truth and wisdom.

Hindu fundamentalists therefore do not claim that there is one literally true sacred text. However, they are less tolerant of other faiths than the majority of Hindus. They believe that India – where 80 per cent of the population is Hindu – should remain Hindu, and are pushing for a change in the **constitution** to limit the freedom of other religions to preach and worship.

Hindu fundamentalism experienced an upsurge in the late 1980s. Many Hindus were concerned about the rise of other religions in India, such as Christianity, Islam, Buddhism and Sikhism. They opposed **secularism** – a policy followed by Indian governments, for the sake of the religious minorities of India – and

'Increasing intolerance among the Hindu fundamentalist organizations, which pose a grave threat to democracy, are an indication of the rise of fascist forces in India. What happened with European fascism is now happening with Hindus.'

M. Mohanty, Professor of Politics, Delhi University, February 2000.

The Dalit

The policy of secularism also threatened the Hindu **caste** system. Under this system people are born into a certain rank in society, depending on the caste (or social grouping) of their family, and this cannot be changed. The lowest ranked caste are the Dalit, or Oppressed. They have few rights or legal protection, and many are forced to live separately from other Hindus. There have been several cases since 1990 where Hindu fundamentalists have shown their 'superiority' over the Dalit by mistreating and even killing them.

wished to create a truly Hindu nation, or *Hindu Rashtra.*

In 1992 in the northern Indian town of Ayodhya a sixteenth-century Muslim mosque, believed to have been built on the site of a Hindu temple, was destroyed by Hindu fundamentalists. The Vishwa Hindu Parishad, a Hindu fundamentalist organization, then led a campaign to build a Hindu temple on the site, causing further anguish to the Muslim community.

In 1999, a Hindu fundamentalist party, the Bharatiya Janata Party (BJP) took power in India. The BJP had previously supported a policy of Hindutva (the establishment of a Hindu state). However, since forming the government, the party has presented a more moderate image to the public. Despite its new image, the BJP has introduced policies to make Indian education more Hindu-based, and history books have been rewritten to emphasize India's Hindu past.

Hindu fundamentalists hold a news conference to publicize their plans to build a temple on the site of the razed mosque at Ayodhya, India.

Buddhist fundamentalism

Buddhism is practised mainly in South-East Asia, as well as by many people in the West. It is a peaceful faith, preaching kindness and compassion to fellow human beings, and it has no sacred text that serves as a guide to life. Despite this, an intolerant, fundamentalist form of Buddhism emerged in the twentieth century. The two main locations of Buddhist fundamentalism are Bhutan in the eastern Himalayas and Sri Lanka.

In Bhutan, the state religion is Buddhism. The ruling monarchy has adopted a very strict and historical form of Buddhism. The king, who shares power with Bhutan's Buddhist monks, has reinterpreted the *Dharma*, or spiritual laws of Buddhism, as a way of strengthening his own authority. He has followed a policy of purging Bhutan of foreign cultures and non-Buddhist religions. The Hindus of southern Bhutan have been forced to adopt Buddhist traditions and culture. In the 1990s they suffered imprisonment and torture for trying to demand equal rights.

On the island of Sri Lanka, Buddhist fundamentalism is practised by the Sinhalese people, who form the majority of the population. In a similar way to the Bhutanese monarchy, the Sinhalese have used Buddhism as a means of reinforcing their power and dominance on the island. Sinhala-Buddhist fundamentalism has proved a mixed blessing for Sri Lanka. It has strengthened Sri Lanka's sense of national identity, but it has also brought conflict between the Sinhalese and the Tamils, an **ethnic minority** in the north-east of the island.

Sikh fundamentalism

The Sikh faith began in India in the fifteenth century. It includes elements of both Hinduism and

A Sinhalese Buddhist monk. Buddhism has been Sri Lanka's main religion since the third century BCE. Buddhist fundamentalists believe that Sri Lanka is destined to be the island of the Dharma, or Buddhist teachings.

Islam, yet it is different from both. Sikhs believe in one god called *Waheguru*, meaning 'Great Teacher'. Equality of all people lies at the heart of their faith, and Sikhs place great emphasis on giving to the poor.

Sikh fundamentalism emerged in 1981, mainly in response to attacks on the Sikh community in India. The movement was led by a Sikh priest called Bhindranwale, who believed in a traditional form of Sikhism, and pressured the Indian government for a separate Sikh state. Bhindranwale and many others died in an Indian attack on the Sikh Golden Temple in Amritsar in 1984. Since then, some Sikh fundamentalists have carried out terrorist attacks against Indian leaders, including kidnappings, bombings and assassinations. Sikh fundamentalists do not seek converts, and most of their energy is focused on keeping their identity and fighting for an independent nation.

Sant Jarnail Singh Bhindranwale (1947-84)

Bhindranwale trained in a Sikh religious school, becoming its head priest in 1971. He preached a strict form of a Sikhism, denouncing drink, drugs and the trimming of hair. In the early 1980s, he campaigned for a separate Sikh state of Khalistan. This led to a violent Sikh-Hindu conflict in Punjab. Along with 500 armed followers, he took refuge in the Golden Temple at Amritsar. He was killed by Indian security forces when they stormed the temple.

Simranjit Singh Mann (second right), a Sikh political leader, was imprisoned under suspicion of masterminding the assassination of Indian prime minister, Indira Gandhi.

Comparing Fundamentalisms

Islamic and Christian fundamentalism are undoubtedly the most powerful fundamentalist movements operating in the world today. This is partly because they are, in terms of numbers, the largest of the world's religions, and so statistically are bound to attract a higher number of extremist followers. Another major reason for the strength of these forms of fundamentalism is that Islam and Christianity are religions that aim to win over the whole world to their way of thinking. Although Judaism (the Jewish religion) also has one God, one sacred text, and one set of laws, there is no impulse in this religion to convert others, and therefore Jewish fundamentalism remains a small-scale movement.

Hinduism and Buddhism have never produced a fundamentalist movement on the scale of Islam or Christianity. This is because these religions have so many different forms – having been influenced by the local cultures of the different countries where they have taken root – and no single movement can realistically claim to represent the true form of either religion.

Catholics believe that the Pope is God's earthly representative. He interprets the laws and principles of the Bible and tells people how to apply them to their daily lives. This leaves little opportunity for separate fundamentalist movements within the Catholic Church.

While each fundamentalist movement has its own distinctive features, they also contain many similarities. One similarity is the timing of their most recent occurrences: there has been a noticeable upsurge in religious fundamentalism since around 1978. At the heart of all these movements is a rejection of the global trend towards **secularism**.

Attitudes towards democracy

Along with secularism, most fundamentalist movements also reject the idea of democracy – the rule of the people. They propose instead that countries should be ruled by religious leaders. Islamic and Jewish fundamentalists desire new states to be formed based on religious laws – the *shari'ah* and the **halakah** respectively – and the fundamentalist interpretations of these law systems do not allow any role for the will of the people.

Roman Catholics and fundamentalism

Why do we never hear about Catholic fundamentalists? The reason for this absence lies in the nature of the religion. In the Roman Catholic faith, it is the Pope and his advisors who interpret the will of God, and direct Church policy on different issues. By contrast, Protestants and Muslims are encouraged to read the holy scriptures and interpret the will of God in their own way. This has led to a number of separate movements arising within these religions, including fundamentalist groups. There are certainly different shades of belief within Catholicism, from liberal to **conservative**. However, Catholics by definition must accept the authority of the Pope. A Catholic wishing to form a separate movement would first have to leave the Catholic Church.

In the Philippines, armed members of the Muslim fundamentalist group Abu Sayyaf pose for a photograph.

Hindu fundamentalists wish to impose a strict interpretation of Hinduism that would give few rights to members of the lower **castes**. Buddhism has been reinterpreted by its fundamentalist supporters to imply the absolute authority of the king, and Sikh fundamentalists have also adopted a very strict and intolerant form of Sikhism which they would be likely to impose on any future Sikh state.

The Sikh fundamentalist leader Bhindranwale justified the use of violence with the following saying:

'For a Sikh it is a sin to keep weapons and kill anyone, but it is an even greater sin to have weapons and not to seek justice.'

American Christian fundamentalists, by contrast, accept the **democratic** system of the USA, and do not argue for its overthrow. There is no Christian equivalent of the *shari'ah* or the *halakah* which they would seek to impose in place of the US **constitution**. They wish instead to defeat secularism and bring religion back into public life through legal and democratic means. However, many Christian fundamentalist policies are, by their nature, undemocratic because they seek to restrict the rights of certain groups in American society. For example, they wish to ban the practice of homosexuality, and would forbid the teaching of evolution by biology teachers in schools.

Attitudes towards violence

At the heart of most of the world's religions are messages of love, peace and goodwill. Yet religious fundamentalists have always found ways to justify the use of violence. The level of violence that fundamentalists use varies greatly according to their cultural background and the particular circumstances they find themselves in. Christian fundamentalists generally operate within an established democracy – the USA – where they are given plentiful opportunities to press their case without resorting to acts of violence. Among such groups, violence is therefore very rare.

Among Muslim nations, however, there is only one democracy (Turkey), and Islamic fundamentalists, lacking other means of expressing themselves, often resort to bullets and bombs. Jewish fundamentalists live in a democracy (Israel), yet one that has been under threat of attack from hostile neighbours for the whole of its short existence. It is the tension this has caused in Israeli society that has led them to engage in acts of violence.

Both Sikh and Hindu traditions allow violence to be used in situations of self-defence. Hindu fundamentalists use the argument that they are defending their religion and culture from outside threats. One of the first acts of the fundamentalist BJP when it came to government in India in 1999 was to detonate a nuclear bomb to demonstrate the extent of its power.

Sikh boys with blue turbans and curved swords. Sikhs emphasize the importance of defending their religion. The swords and turbans remind Sikhs that they must be ready to fight for their faith.

The Future of Fundamentalism

For as long as there are people who wish to apply the teachings of the scriptures to their daily lives, and try to make others do so as well, fundamentalism will continue to exist. The question is, will fundamentalism always remain on the sidelines, attempting to influence those in power, or will it one day take centre stage?

Protest movement or future government?
American society is now firmly multi-ethnic and multi-religious, with values of tolerance that reflect this, and women and homosexuals will not be persuaded to give up the rights and freedoms they

Supporters hold up a placard of Mohammad Khatami, Iran's moderate, reformist president, during an election rally in February 2000. The fundamentalist rulers of Iran suffered a major defeat in that election, when reformists won control of the Iranian parliament.

Fundamentalist Christianity in Africa

The twentieth century witnessed a shift of Christianity from being a religion practised by a majority of white people, to one that is followed by a non-white majority. In the early twenty-first century, more than 60 per cent of Christians are from Africa, Asia and Latin America. This has come about largely through the **missionary** efforts of the Evangelical Protestant church. It is possible that these places may prove a future source for Christian fundamentalism.

have fought so hard to win. The Christian fundamentalists have instead resigned themselves to the status of a protest group, campaigning and demonstrating on specific issues and concerns.

Islamic fundamentalism – as the most potent and aggressive form of fundamentalism in the world today – is likely to remain a considerable force in Muslim societies. However, the chances are it will not succeed in its overall objective, which is the overthrow of nations, and the re-establishment of the **caliphate**. The idea of the nation has proved a strong one, and even in places where fundamentalists have taken power, they have failed in their attempts to export the revolution to Muslims in other countries.

Islamic fundamentalism has faced several setbacks since the mid-1990s. In Iran, the strict regime of the *ayatollahs* became increasingly unpopular, leading to the election of a moderate government in 1997. In Sudan, the government's leading fundamentalist, Hassan al-Turabi, was forced out of office in 2000. The fundamentalist Wahhabi monarchy in Saudi Arabia has faced calls for greater freedom and democracy from human rights groups, such as the Saudi Committee for the Defence of Legitimate Rights (SCDLR) and the Movement for Islamic Reform in Arabia (MIRA).

57

Nevertheless, as a pressure group in Muslim society, Islamic fundamentalism still flourishes. The United States' war on terror and the escalating Israel–Palestine conflict has revived Islamic militancy, especially in the Middle East and central and southern Asia. So long as the USA and the West appear to be pursuing aggressive policies towards Muslims, the terrorists of Al Qaeda, Hamas and Islamic Jihad will find an audience for their message of hate.

While the terrorist groups try to influence world opinion with suicide bombs and hijackings, there is another, quieter movement going on, influencing Muslim society at a deeper level. Some predict that the future for Islamic fundamentalism will not be about violent change, but about the day-to-day efforts by members of Islamic groups to make Muslim countries more religious. For example, the Muslim Brotherhood is active in Egypt with campaigns to ban alcohol, **pornography** and TV satellite dishes, and impose stricter dress codes. In Lebanon, Jordan and Kuwait, fundamentalists wage court battles and press campaigns against 'un-Islamic' writers and artists.

This Egyptian version of the popular quiz show, 'Who Wants to Be a Millionaire?' demonstrates how the Arab world continues to be influenced by Western culture, despite the efforts of the fundamentalists. In July 2001, the conservative religious authorities issued a *fatwah* condemning the show as sinful and a form of gambling.

'Countries [in the Middle East] with secular governments are more religious than they were even twenty years ago. And so these movements, instead of being revolutionary, are becoming evolutionary, pushing for incremental [gradual] change.'

Michael Dunn, editor of the *Middle East Journal*, March 2000.

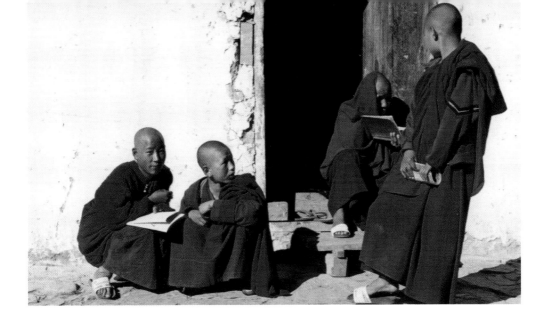

Fundamentalists in power

There are places in the world where fundamentalism has managed to take centre stage, in countries like Iran, Bhutan and Saudi Arabia. Fundamentalists achieved success in these countries because most of their populations were deeply religious and had little experience of **secularism**. Yet each of these regimes has had difficulties in keeping out Western and **secular** influences. They have remained in power either because they have gradually softened their fundamentalist principles, or – in the case of Bhutan – because they have made themselves a completely closed society.

It is likely that future fundamentalists – if they achieve power – will be faced with this kind of choice. If their people are able to interact with Western democracies, they will encounter greater freedoms for women and **ethnic minorities**, as well as freedom of worship. Some may dislike these freedoms, and be offended by Western liberal attitudes, but others will be attracted to them, and this will always cause problems for fundamentalist regimes.

Bhutanese children doing their school homework. Since Bhutan closed its doors to outside influence, its people have become among the poorest in the world.

'There is no clash of civilizations between Islam and the West. The really decisive battle is taking place <u>within</u> Muslim civilization, where ultra-conservatives compete against moderates and democrats for the soul of the Muslim public.'

Robert W. Hefner, Department of Anthropology, Boston University, USA, May 2002.

Date List

1730s–50s	The First Great Awakening.
1736	Al-Wahhab begins to preach his message of Islamic revivalism.
1745–1800	Wahhabism spreads throughout the Arabian peninsula.
1800–1830s	The Second Great Awakening.
1830s–40s	The start of the American millenarian movement.
1859	Publication of Darwin's *The Origin of Species* which sparked the 'evolution' controversy.
1875	Formation of the Islamic Movement.
1897	First Zionist conference held in Basle, Switzerland.
1902	Founding of the American Bible League to promote the Bible as a work of literal truth.
1910–15	Publication of *The Fundamentals of the Faith* by a group of conservative Protestants.
1917	Balfour Declaration: Britain promises support in the establishment of a homeland for Jewish people in Israel.
1918	Collapse of the Ottoman Empire.
1919	Millenarians change their name to World's Christian Fundamentals Association.
1920	The term 'fundamentalism' is invented.
1922	Harry Emerson Fosdick gives influential sermon, 'Shall the Fundamentalists Win?'
1925	Scopes trial.
1928	Formation of the Muslim Brotherhood, an Islamic revivalist group, in Egypt.
1930s–40s	Period of consolidation for Christian fundamentalism.
1938	The Muslim Brotherhood begins to engage in terrorism.
1948	The establishment of the state of Israel. 750,000 Palestinian Arabs become refugees.
1950s–60s	Emergence of the Christian Evangelical movement.
1960–66	Sayyid Qutb writes his influential works on the creation of a pure Islamic state.
1967	Israel defeats Arab forces in the Six Day War. Israeli territory expands to include the West Bank and Gaza Strip.
1968	The PLO turns to terrorism.
1973	Abortion is made legal in the United States.
1974	Establishment of the Jewish fundamentalist group Gush Emunim.
1975–88	The era of the Moral Majority and the televangelists.
1978	Formation of Hamas, an Islamic fundamentalist terrorist group.
1979	A revolution in Iran brings the fundamentalist regime of Ayatollah Khomeini to power.
1980	Gush Emunim turns to terrorism.
1980s–90s	A period of widespread Islamic militancy and terrorism.

1981	Emergence of Sikh fundamentalism.	1992	Hindu fundamentalists destroy Muslim mosque.
1982	President Sadat of Egypt is assassinated by Islamic fundamentalists.	1994	29 Muslims killed by Jewish fundamentalist, Baruch Goldstein.
1984	Indian troops attack Sikh Golden Temple in Amritsar, killing many including the fundamentalist Sikh leader, Bhindranwale.	1995	Israel's prime minister assassinated by a Jewish fundamentalist.

1981 Emergence of Sikh fundamentalism.

1982 President Sadat of Egypt is assassinated by Islamic fundamentalists.

1984 Indian troops attack Sikh Golden Temple in Amritsar, killing many including the fundamentalist Sikh leader, Bhindranwale.

1988 Christian fundamentalist Pat Robertson campaigns for the Republican candidacy for US president.

1988 Upsurge of Hindu fundamentalism.

1989 Ayatollah Khomeini issues a *fatwah* against Salman Rushdie.

1989 A fundamentalist regime comes to power in Sudan under Hassan al-Turabi and Omar Hassan al-Bashir.

1989 The formation of the Christian Coalition.

1990 Jewish fundamentalist leader Meir Kahane is assassinated.

1992 Hindu fundamentalists destroy Muslim mosque.

1994 29 Muslims killed by Jewish fundamentalist, Baruch Goldstein.

1995 Israel's prime minister assassinated by a Jewish fundamentalist.

1995–2001 The Taleban rules Afghanistan.

1997 A reformist government is elected in Iran.

1998 Osama bin Laden issues his *fatwah* calling for Americans to be killed.

1999 The BJP, a Hindu fundamentalist party, takes power in India.

2001 Passenger planes are flown into buildings in the United States killing more than 3,000 people. The attacks are organized by the Islamic fundamentalist group, Al Qaeda.

2002 More than 180 people are killed in a bomb blast at a nightclub in Bali, Indonesia. The attack is blamed on local Islamic terrorists with possible links to Al Qaeda.

Resources

Books

Fundamentalism, Steve Bruce, Polity Press, 2000

21st Century Debates: Terrorism, Alex Woolf, Hodder Wayland, 2003

What's at Issue: War and Conflict, Sean Connolly, Heinemann Library, 2002

Troubled World: The Arab-Israeli Conflict, Ivan Minnis, Heinemann Library, 2001

Religions of the World, Elizabeth Breuilly, Joanne O'Brien, Martin Palmer, Hodder Wayland, 1997

A New Handbook of Living Religions, John R. Hinnells (ed.), Penguin Books, 1998

Glossary

anti-modern movement
a movement that is opposed to the culture, technology and social changes of modern society.

baptism
a religious ceremony in which the person being baptized is sprinkled with or immersed in water to symbolize purification.

Bible
the sacred book of the Christian religion. The Old Testament of the Bible, or Hebrew Bible, is a sacred book of the Jewish religion.

burka
an all-over garment with veiled eyeholes, worn by some Muslim women.

caliphate
the territory over which a caliph's rule extends, or the time for which it lasts.

caste
any of the four main hereditary classes into which Hindu society is divided. A person's caste determines his or her social status.

conservative
a follower of conservatism – a political or religious philosophy based on a desire to keep things as they are, and to preserve traditional ways of life and behaviour.

constitution
a written document outlining the basic laws or principles by which a country is governed.

creation science
the attempt to provide scientific proof for the account of God's creation of the world as described in the Bible.

creed
a set of religious beliefs.

Democrat
a member of the Democratic Party, one of the two major political parties of the USA.

democratic
used to describe a system of government where the leaders have been elected freely and equally by all its citizens, or a country with such a system.

Dharma
the teachings of the Buddha.

doctrine
a rule or principle that forms the basis of a religious belief.

ethnic minority
a group with a similar cultural background that forms a minority in a country.

evolution, theory of
a theory by which all species, including humans, develop from earlier forms of life.

exploitative
making unfair use of somebody.

gender roles
the different parts that men and women are expected to play in society.

Hadith
a collection of the sayings of Muhammad, the founder of Islam, and stories about his life. The Hadith is a source of guidance for Muslims.

halakah
the body of Jewish law, beginning with the first five books of the Hebrew Bible, and developed by rabbis.

hereditary
a system in which the leadership of a country, religion or other institution is passed on from one generation to the next.

immigrant
a person who moves from one country to settle in another.

Industrial Revolution
the period beginning in the second half of the eighteenth century when Britain, Europe and the USA experienced a surge in productivity and wealth due to the widespread adoption of large scale, mechanical means of production.

jihad
the struggle for Islam. This can be interpreted either as a holy war, or as a spiritual striving.

legislation
the process of making laws.

liberalism
a belief in freedom of thought, speech, action and religion, and tolerance towards others.

literal
exactly following the meaning of an original word or text.

lobby
to try to influence those people making laws.

meditation
the emptying of the mind of thoughts, or concentration on just one thing, to aid spiritual development.

militant
extremely active in support of a cause, often to an extent that causes conflict with other people or institutions.

millenarian movement
a movement that believed in Jesus Christ's Second Coming, a final conflict between good and evil, and the end of the world, based on the biblical book of Revelation.

missionary
somebody sent on a religious mission to spread the faith or to do social and medical work.

mosque
a building in which Muslims worship.

nationalism
belief in the right of one's people to exist as a nation, or belief in the status of one's nation above all others.

natural selection
the process by which creatures best suited to survival in a particular environment find it easier to find a sexual partner, and pass on their characteristics to future generations. This, according to Charles Darwin, is how evolution works.

orator
someone who speaks to a public audience.

Ottoman Empire
a Turkish empire established in the late thirteenth century in Asia Minor, eventually extending through the Middle East. The Ottoman Empire came to an end in 1922.

Pentecostal
belonging to a Christian denomination that emphasizes the workings of the Holy Spirit and interprets the Bible literally.

pornography
sexually explicit films, magazines, photographs and other materials.

primates
mammals with large brains and complex hands and feet, including humans, apes and monkeys.

rabbi
a Jewish religious leader, or scholar qualified to interpret Jewish law.

racial integration
the process of opening a community to all, regardless of racial background.

radicalism
belief in extreme political, economic or social change.

Ramadan
the ninth month of the Islamic calendar, during which Muslims fast.

revivalist movement
a movement within a religion to reawaken religious commitment.

salvation
in the Christian religion this means deliverance from sin through the sacrifice of Jesus Christ, or through personal acceptance of Christ.

secular
not concerned with religious matters.

secularism
the belief that religion should play no part in political life, and should be not be involved in running public institutions, especially schools.

Talmud
the collection of ancient Jewish writings that makes up the basis of Jewish religious law.

televangelism
a form of Christian evangelism in which the services are broadcast on television.

Torah
the first five books of the Hebrew Bible, written on a parchment scroll for use in services in synagogues (Jewish places of worship).

Wahhabism
a very conservative movement within Islam that rejects any innovation that occurred after the third century of Islam.

Zionism
a worldwide movement that sought to establish a Jewish nation in Palestine. Since 1948, Zionists continue to act in support of Israel.

Index